W9-CPF-869

My First Book of
COWBOY SONGS

My First Book of
COWBOY SONGS

21 Favorite Songs in Easy Piano Arrangements

Dolly M. Moon
Assistant Director, The Music School, Brooklyn, N.Y.

With Illustrations by
FREDERIC REMINGTON

DOVER PUBLICATIONS, INC.
NEW YORK

This book is dedicated to the memory of Sasha Backer, who was a student at The Music School 1977-78.

Copyright © 1982 by Dolly M. Moon.
All rights reserved under Pan American and International Copyright Conventions.

Published in Canada by General Publishing Company, Ltd., 30 Lesmill Road, Don Mills, Toronto, Ontario.
Published in the United Kingdom by Constable and Company, Ltd., 3 The Lanchesters, 162-164 Fulham Palace Road, London W6 9ER.

My First Book of Cowboy Songs is a retitled republication of *My Very First Book of Cowboy Songs: 21 Favorite Songs in Easy Piano Arrangements,* first published by Dover Publications, Inc., in 1982.

International Standard Book Number: 0-486-24311-7

Manufactured in the United States of America
Dover Publications, Inc.
31 East 2nd Street
Mineola, N.Y. 11501

Contents

	page
Goodbye, Ol' Paint	1
Ev'ry Night When the Sun Goes In	2
I'm Going to Leave Old Texas	3
Red River Valley	4
My Darling Clementine (four hands)	6
Down in the Valley	9
She'll Be Coming 'Round the Mountain	10
Sweet Betsy from Pike	12
The Cowboy	14
Strawberry Roan	15
The Boll Weevil	18
On Top of Old Smoky	20
My Home's in Montana	21
Nelly Bly (four hands)	22
The Lone Prairie	25
Shenandoah	26
Home on the Range	28
Here, Rattler, Here (four hands)	30
The Rainbow Cradle	33
Nebraska Boys	34
The Streets of Laredo	36

Goodbye, Ol' Paint

Cowboy Song

Ev'ry Night When the Sun Goes In

American

I'm Going to Leave Old Texas

I'm going to leave old Tex - as now.

They've no more use for the long-horned cow.

2. They've plowed and fenced my cattle range,
And the people there are all so strange.

Red River Valley

American Song

Dm
C7
F
has - ten to bid me a - dieu. Just re - mem - ber the Red Riv - er
Bb
F
C7
F
Val - ley, and the one who has loved you so true.

My Darling Clementine

(secondo)

Traditional

My Darling Clementine

(primo)

Traditional

2. Light she was, and like a fairy,
   And her shoes were number nine;
   Herring boxes without topses
   Sandals were for Clementine.

3. Drove she ducklings to the water
   Ev'ry morning just at nine;
   Hit her foot against a splinter,
   Fell into the foaming brine.

4. Ruby lips above the water,
   Blowing bubbles soft and fine;
   But, alas, I was no swimmer,
   So I lost my Clementine.

5. Then the miner, forty-niner,
   Soon began to peak and pine;
   Thought he oughter join his daughter.
   Now he's with his Clementine.

6. In my dreams she still does haunt me,
   Robed in garments soaked in brine;
   Though in life I used to hug her,
   Now she's dead, I draw the line.

Remington

Down in the Valley

Kentucky Mountain Song

2. Hear the wind blow, dear, hear the wind blow;
   Hang your head over, hear the wind blow.

She'll Be Coming 'Round the Mountain

American Folk Song

2. She'll be driving six white horses when she comes.
3. We will all go out to meet her when she comes.
4. We will kill the old red rooster when she comes.
5. We will have chicken and dumplings when she comes.
6. She'll be wearing wool pajamas when she comes.
7. She will have to sleep with Grandma when she comes.

Sweet Betsy from Pike

Traditional American

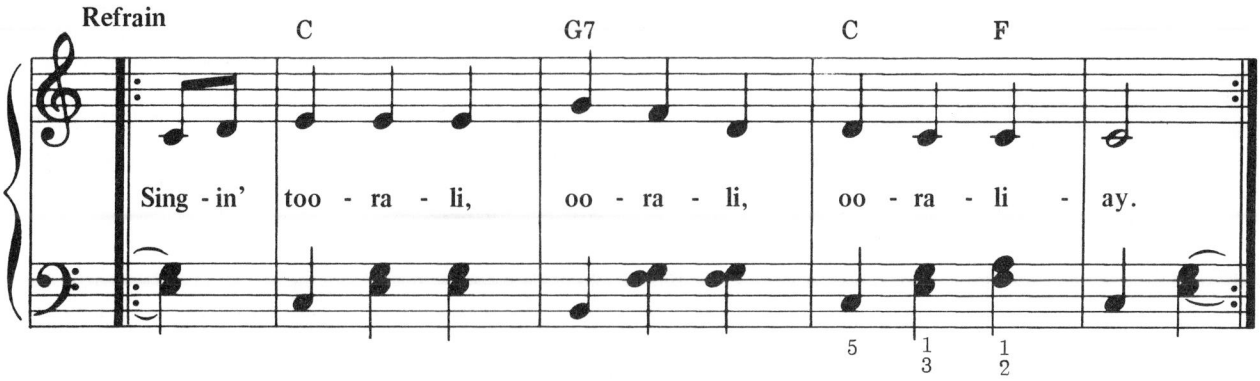

2. The Shanghai ran off and the cattle all died,
   The last piece of bacon that morning was fried;
   Poor Ike got discouraged, and Betsy got mad,
   The dog wagged his tail and looked wonderfully sad.

3. One morning they climbed up a very high hill,
   And with wonder looked down into old Placerville;
   Ike shouted and said, as he cast his eyes down,
   "Sweet Betsy, my darling, we've got to Hangtown."

The Cowboy

Old Texas Melody
Words by MAYME CHRISTENSON

Strawberry Roan

Cowboy Song

Refrain
C
G7
C
Well, it's oh, that straw - ber - ry roan.
F
C
F
Oh, that straw - ber - ry roan. That straw - ber - ry
C
Dm
po - ny no one ev - er rode, and the cow - boy that tries it is
C
G7
C
sure to get thrown! Oh, that straw - ber - ry roan!

2. "You've guessed me just right! I'm your man," I claim.
"Do you have a wild horse you'd like me to tame?"
Well, he said that he had, and a bad one to buck,
And for throwing good riders, the horse had good luck.

3. I jumped on his back and I held the reins;
That strawberry horse threw me off for my pains.
So I climbed on again to the horse's surprise,
And he tried then to throw me right up to the skies.

The Boll Weevil

Texas Folk Song

2. First time I saw the weevil, he's sittin' on the square.
   The next time that I saw him, he had all his family there.
   Just a-lookin' for a home (etc.).

3. Last time I saw the weevil, he'd settled down for life;
   He'd brought his aunts and uncles, his cousin and his wife.
   They're a-lookin' for a home (etc.).

On Top of Old Smoky

Kentucky Mountain Song

2. A-courting is pleasure, and parting is grief,
But a false-hearted lover is worse than a thief.

My Home's in Montana

Cowboy Song

Nelly Bly

(secondo)

STEPHEN FOSTER

Chorus

Nelly Bly

(primo)

STEPHEN FOSTER

2. Nelly Bly has a voice like the turtle dove;
I hear it in the meadow, and I hear it in the grove.
Nelly Bly has a heart warm as a cup of tea,
And bigger than the sweet potato down in Tennessee.

3. Nelly Bly shuts her eyes when she goes to sleep,
And when she wakens up again her eyeballs 'gin to peep.
The way she walks, she lifts her foot, and then she puts it down,
And when it falls there's music there in that part of the town.

4. Nelly Bly, Nelly Bly! Never, never sigh.
Never bring the teardrop to the corner of your eye.
For the pie is made of pumpkins, and the mush is made of corn,
And there's corn and pumpkins plenty, love, a-lyin' in the barn.

The Lone Prairie

Traditional

2. "Oh, bury me not on the lone prairie
Where the coyotes howl and the wind blows free.
In a cold, cold grave don't bury me,
Oh, bury me not on the lone prairie."

3. "Oh, bury me not—" and his voice failed there.
But we took no heed of his dying prayer;
In a narrow grave just six by three
We buried him there on the lone prairie.

Shenandoah

Traditional

2. Oh, Shenandoah, I love your daughter.
   Way, hey, you rolling river!
   Oh, Shenandoah, I love your daughter.
   Way, hey, we're bound away
   'Cross the wide Missouri.

3. Oh, Shenandoah, I'm bound to leave you.
   Way, hey, you rolling river!
   Oh, Shenandoah, I'll not deceive you.
   Way, hey, we're bound away
   'Cross the wide Missouri.

Home on the Range

Cowboy Song

Refrain
5
C7
F
1
4
Home, home on the range where deer and
B♭
C7
1
F
3
F7
an - te - lope play. Where sel - dom is heard a dis -
B♭
B♭
F
C7
F
cour - ag - ing word, and skies are not cloud - y all day.

Here, Rattler, Here

(secondo)

American Folk Song

Refrain

Here, Rattler, Here

2. Oh, once I had a setting hen, set her as you know;
   Set her on six dozen eggs and hatched out one old crow.

3. Old Rattler's dead and gone, alas, gone where good dogs go.
   Better watch out and don't play dog, or you'll be a goner, too.

The Rainbow Cradle

Navajo Indian Song

2. Rainbows lie beneath you, downy clouds around you.
Hush, my little white shell; do not cry, my white shell.
Go to sleep, my white shell; go to sleep, my white shell.

Nebraska Boys

American Folk Song

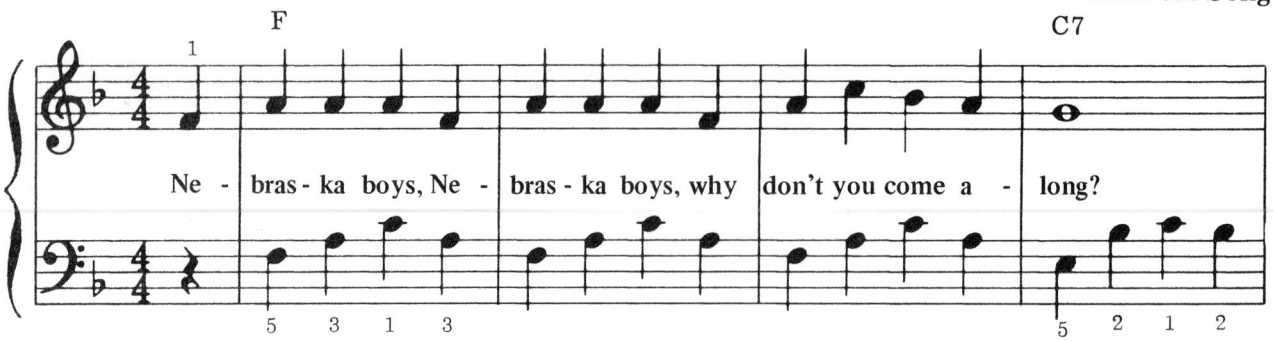

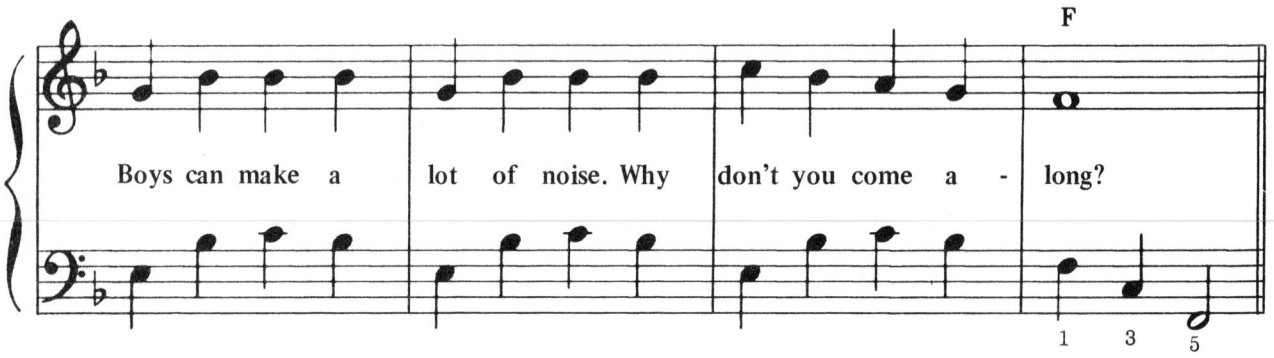

Refrain

2. Nebraska girls, Nebraska girls, why don't you come along?
Sky-blue eyes and pretty curls. Why don't you come along?

The Streets of Laredo

Traditional

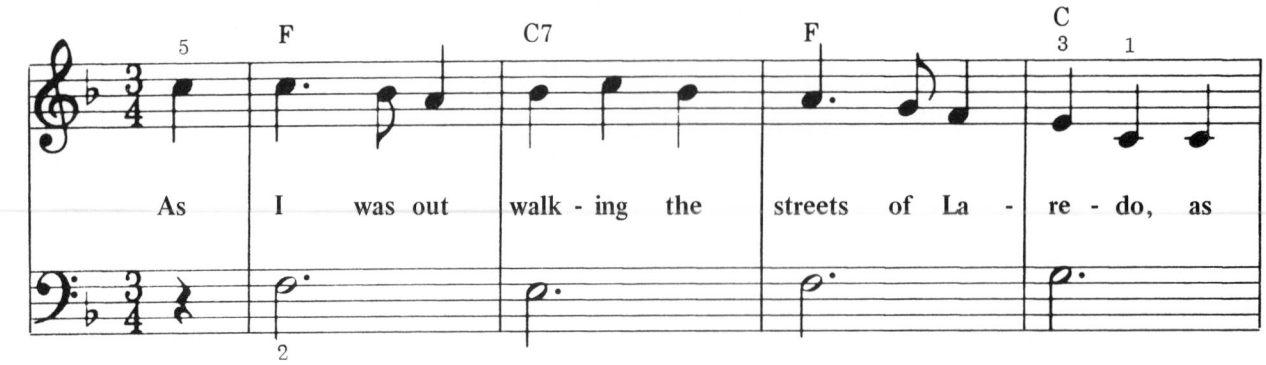

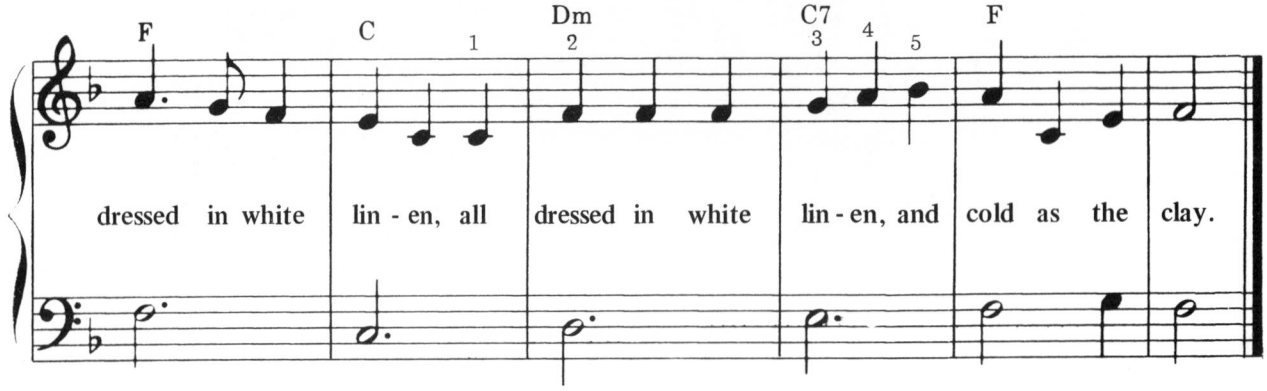

2. "I see by your outfit that you are a cowboy,"
These words he did say as I boldly stepped by.
"Come sit down beside me and hear my sad story;
I was shot in the breast and I know I must die."

3. "O beat the drum slowly and play the fife lowly,
And play the dead march as you bear me along.
Take me to the green valley and lay the sod o'er me,
For I'm a young cowboy and I know I've done wrong."